THE COMPLETE ORGAN PLAYER POP SONGBOOK

CONTENTS

SONGS

Wise Publications
London/New York/Sydney/Cologne

Exclusive Distributors:
Music Sales Limited
78 Newman Street, London W1P 3LA, England
Music Sales Pty. Limited
27 Clarendon Street, Artarmon, Sydney, NSW 2064, Australia

Designed by Howard Brown
Arranged and compiled by Kenneth Baker

Music Sales complete catalogue lists thousands of
titles and is free from your local music book shop,
or direct from Music Sales Limited.
Please send 30p in stamps for postage to
Music Sales Limited, 78 Newman Street, London W1P 3LA.

Printed in England by
J.B. Offset Printers (Marks Tey) Limited, Marks Tey.

REGISTRATION TABLE
(For All Organs)

GENERAL ELECTRONIC ORGANS

(1) Upper: Saxophone 8', or Trumpet 8'
+ Wow (if available)
Lower: Orchestral Strings
Pedal: Bass Guitar 8'
Vibrato: On

(2) Upper: Guitar (or Flute 16' + 4',
$2^2/_3$' percussion)
Lower: Flutes 8', 4'
Pedal: Bass Guitar 8'
Vibrato: Off. Leslie Chorale optional

(3) Upper: Piano (or Electric Piano)
Lower: Flutes 8', 4'
Pedal: 8'
Vibrato: Off. Leslie: Chorale

(4) Upper: Orchestral Strings
Lower: Flutes 8', 4'
Pedal: 16' + 8'
Vibrato: On (Leslie Tremolo with
Flutes)

(5) Upper: Synthesized brass (or
Trombone 16', Trumpet 8')
Lower: Flute 8', String 8'
Pedal: 16' + 8'
Vibrato: On

(6) Upper: Flutes 16', 8', 4', 2'
Lower: Flute 8', String 8'
Pedal: 16' + 8'
Vibrato: Off. Leslie: Tremolo

(7) Upper: Flutes 16', 8', 4', Trumpet 8'
Lower: Flutes 8', 4', Horn 8'
Pedal: 16' + 8'
Vibrato: Off. Leslie: Tremolo

(8) Upper: Flutes 16', 8', 2'
+ Orchestral Strings
Lower: Flutes 8', 4'
Pedal: 16' + 8'
Vibrato: On

DRAWBAR ORGANS

(1) Upper: 00 2478 500
Lower: (00)7642 220(0)
Pedal: 4 – (2)
Vibrato: On

(2) Upper: 80 0000 000 + 3rd Harmonic
Lower: (00)7600 000(0)
Pedal: 4 – (2)
Vibrato: Off. Leslie Chorale optional

(3) Upper: 00 8606 000 + Sustain
Lower: (00)7604 000(0)
Pedal: 5 – (3)
Vibrato: Off. Leslie: Chorale

(4) Upper: 83 5666 333
Lower: (00)8706 000(0)
Pedal: 6 – (4)
Vibrato: On

(5) Upper: 88 8800 000
Lower: (00)8643 210(0)
Pedal: 6 – (4)
Vibrato: On

(6) Upper: 80 8606 006
Lower: (00)8754 322(0)
Pedal: 6 – (3)
Vibrato: Off. Leslie: Tremolo

(7) Upper: 80 8866 000
Lower: (00)7652 000(0)
Pedal: 5 – (3)
Vibrato: Off. Leslie: Tremolo

(8) Upper: 85 5645 444
Lower: (00)8706 000(0)
Pedal: 6 – (3)
Vibrato: On

I JUST CALLED TO SAY I LOVE YOU

Words & Music: Stevie Wonder

Registration No. ③
Suggested Drum Rhythm: **Bossa Nova**

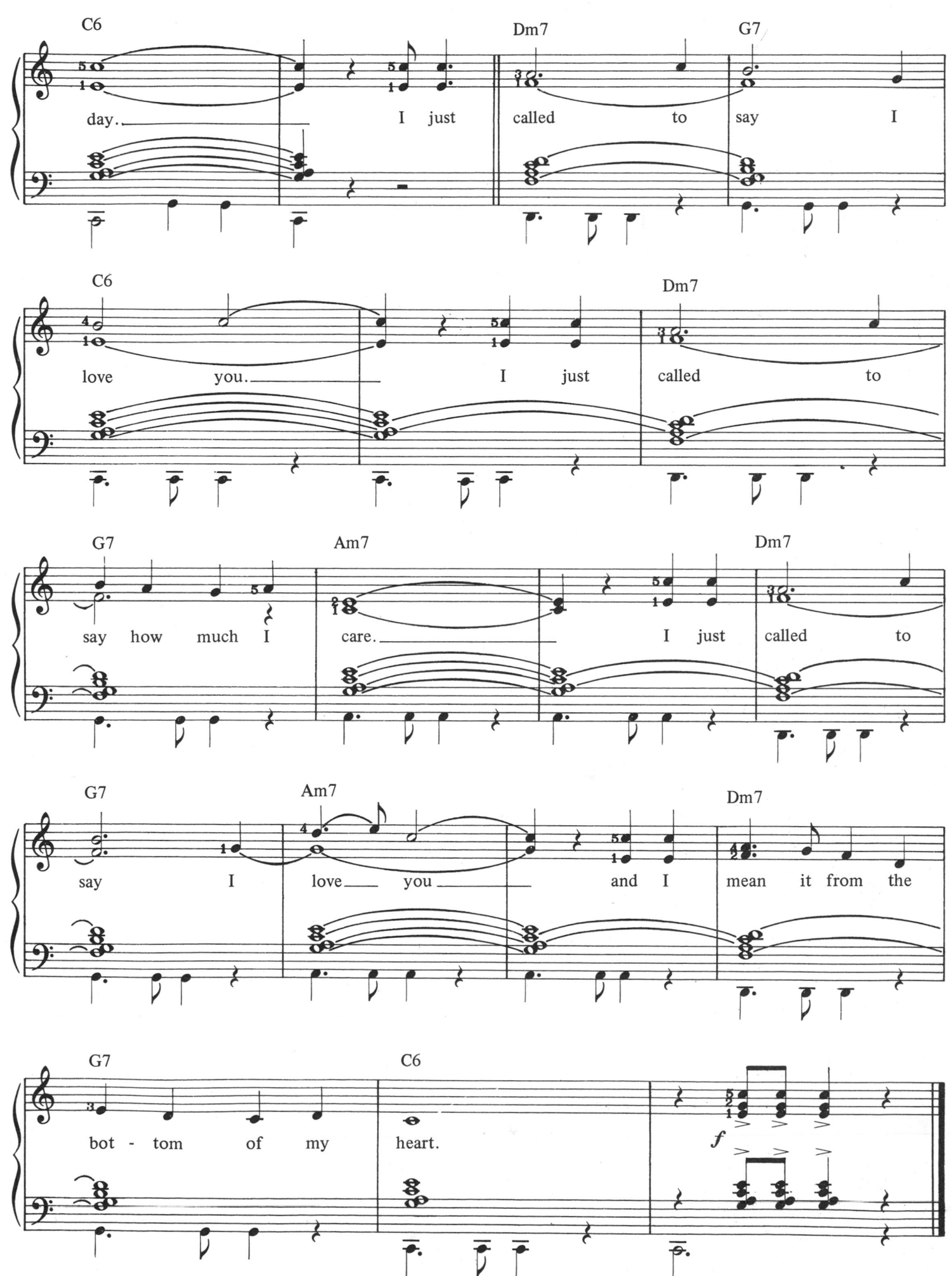

EVERYBODY WANTS TO RULE THE WORLD

Words & Music: Orzabal, Stanley and Hughes

7

TO ALL THE GIRLS I'VE LOVED BEFORE

Words: Hal David
Music: Albert Hammond

Registration No. ④
Suggested Drum Rhythm: **Bossa Nova**

WORDS

Words & Music: R. Fitoussi

Registration No. ⑥
Suggested Drum Rhythm: **Rock**

WHAT'S LOVE GOT TO DO WITH IT

Words & Music: Graham Lyle and Terry Britten

Registration No. ⑦
Suggested Drum Rhythm: **Bossa Nova**

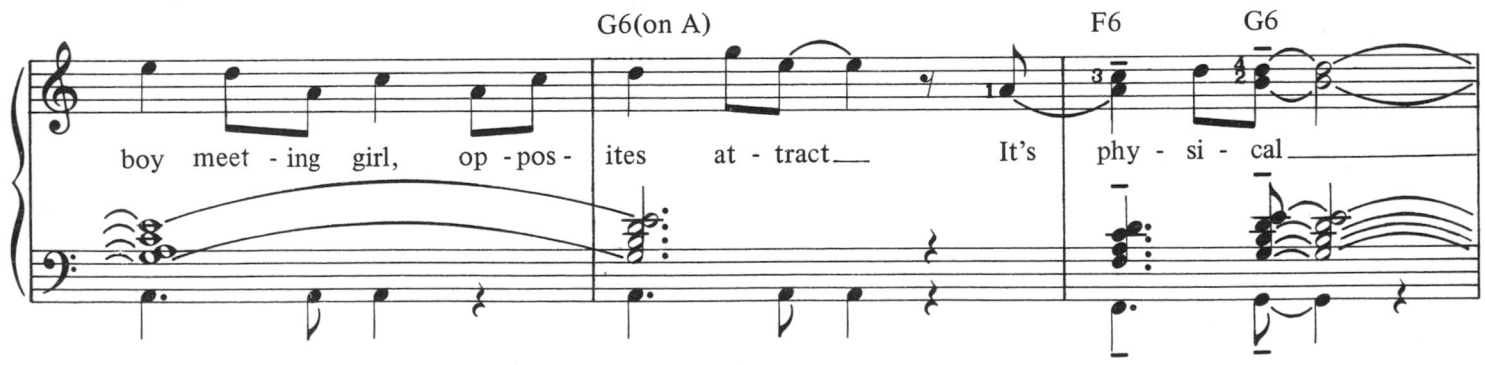

99 RED BALLOONS

Music and Original Lyric: Jorn-Uwe Fahrenkrog-Petersen and Carlos Karges
English Words: Kevin McAlea

Registration No. ②
Suggested Drum Rhythm: **Rock**

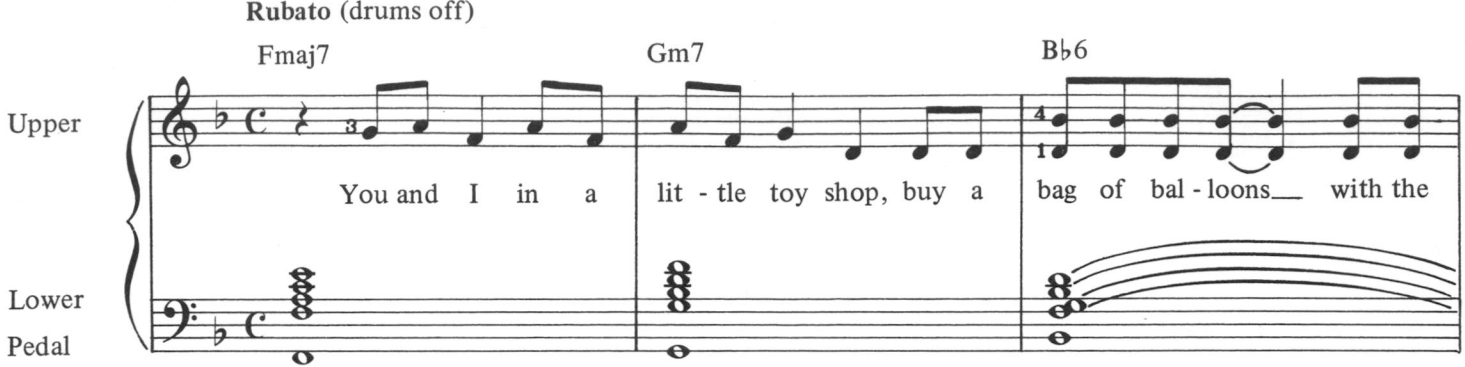

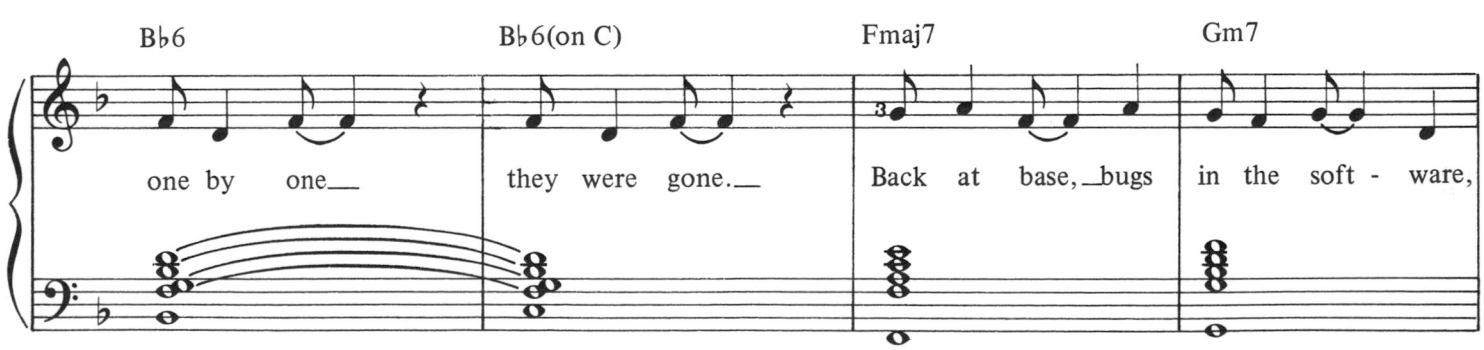

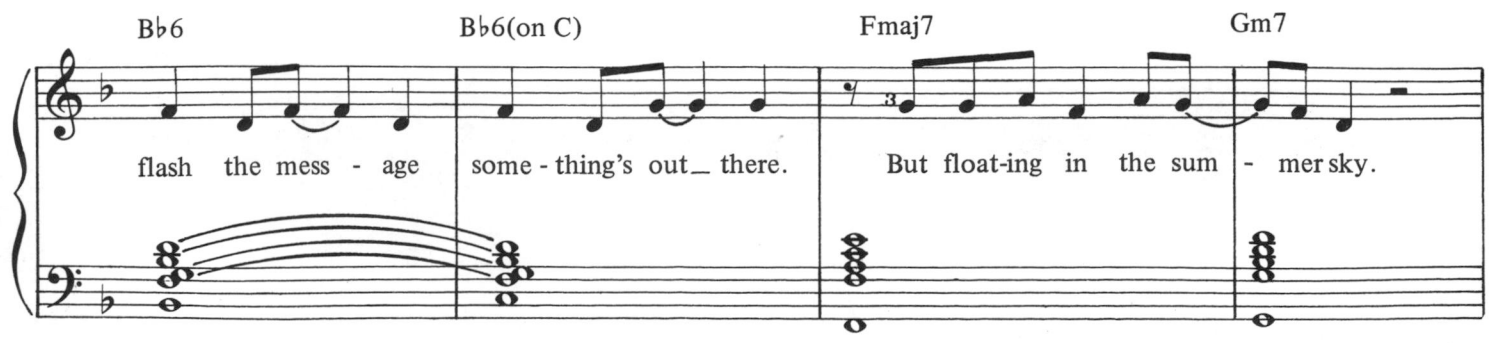

FOOL (IF YOU THINK IT'S OVER)

Words & Music: Chris Rea

Registration No. 8
Suggested Drum Rhythm: **Bossa Nova**

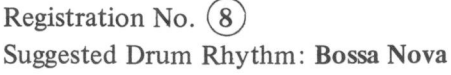

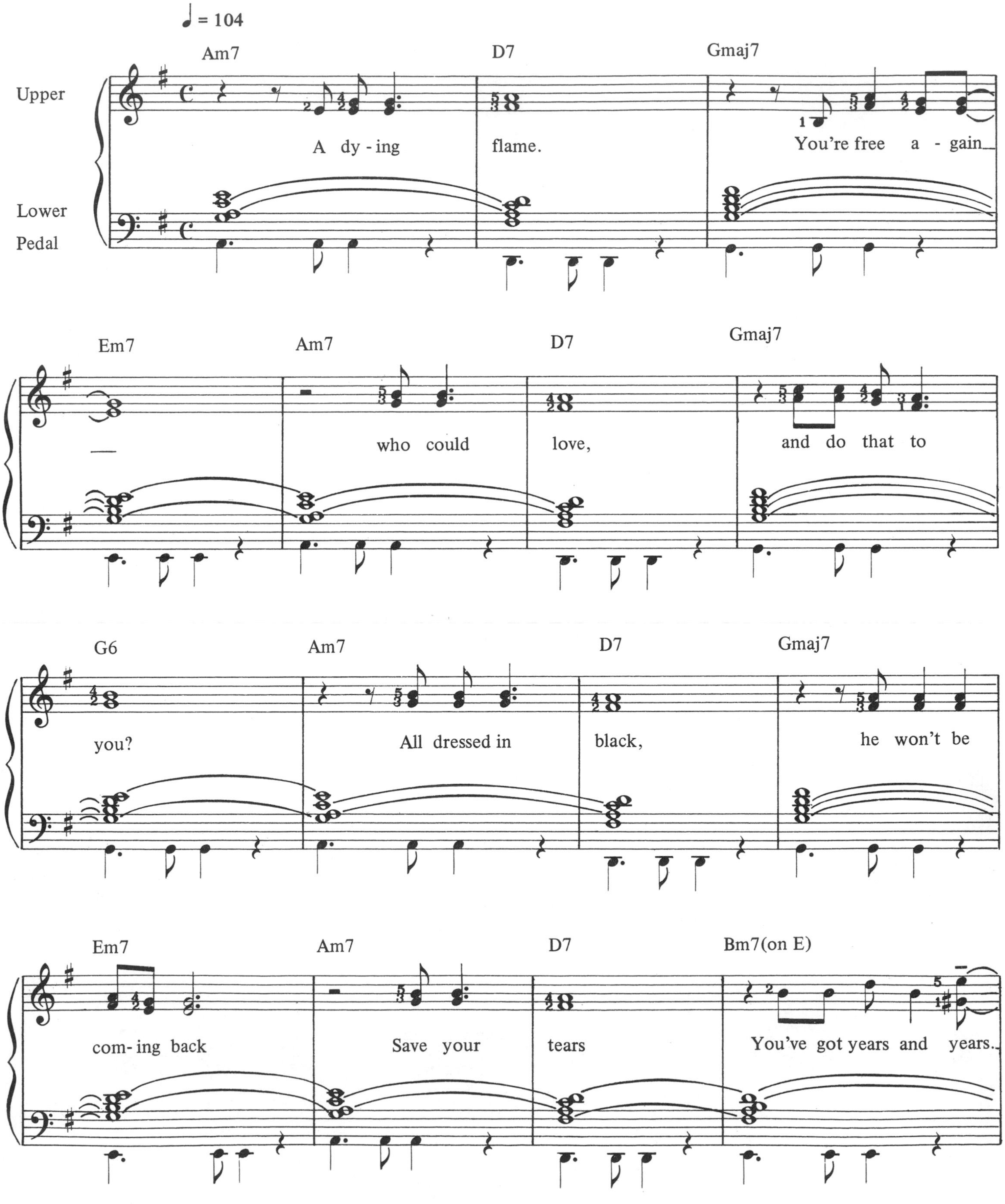

♩ = 104
Upper
Lower
Pedal
Am7
D7
Gmaj7
A dy - ing
flame.
You're free a - gain
Em7
Am7
D7
Gmaj7
who could
love,
and do that to
G6
Am7
D7
Gmaj7
you?
All dressed in
black,
he won't be
Em7
Am7
D7
Bm7(on E)
com- ing back
Save your
tears
You've got years and years.

WHEN YOU'RE YOUNG AND IN LOVE

Words & Music: Van McCoy

Registration No. ⑤
Suggested Drum Rhythm: **Bossa Nova**

GOOD YEAR FOR THE ROSES

Words & Music: Jerry Chesnut

Registration No. ⑥
Suggested Drum Rhythm: **Swing**

KARMA CHAMELEON

Words & Music: O'Dowd, Moss, Hay, Craig and Pickett

Registration No. (1)
Suggested Drum Rhythm: **Rock**

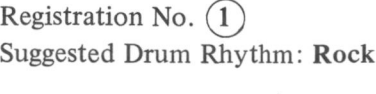

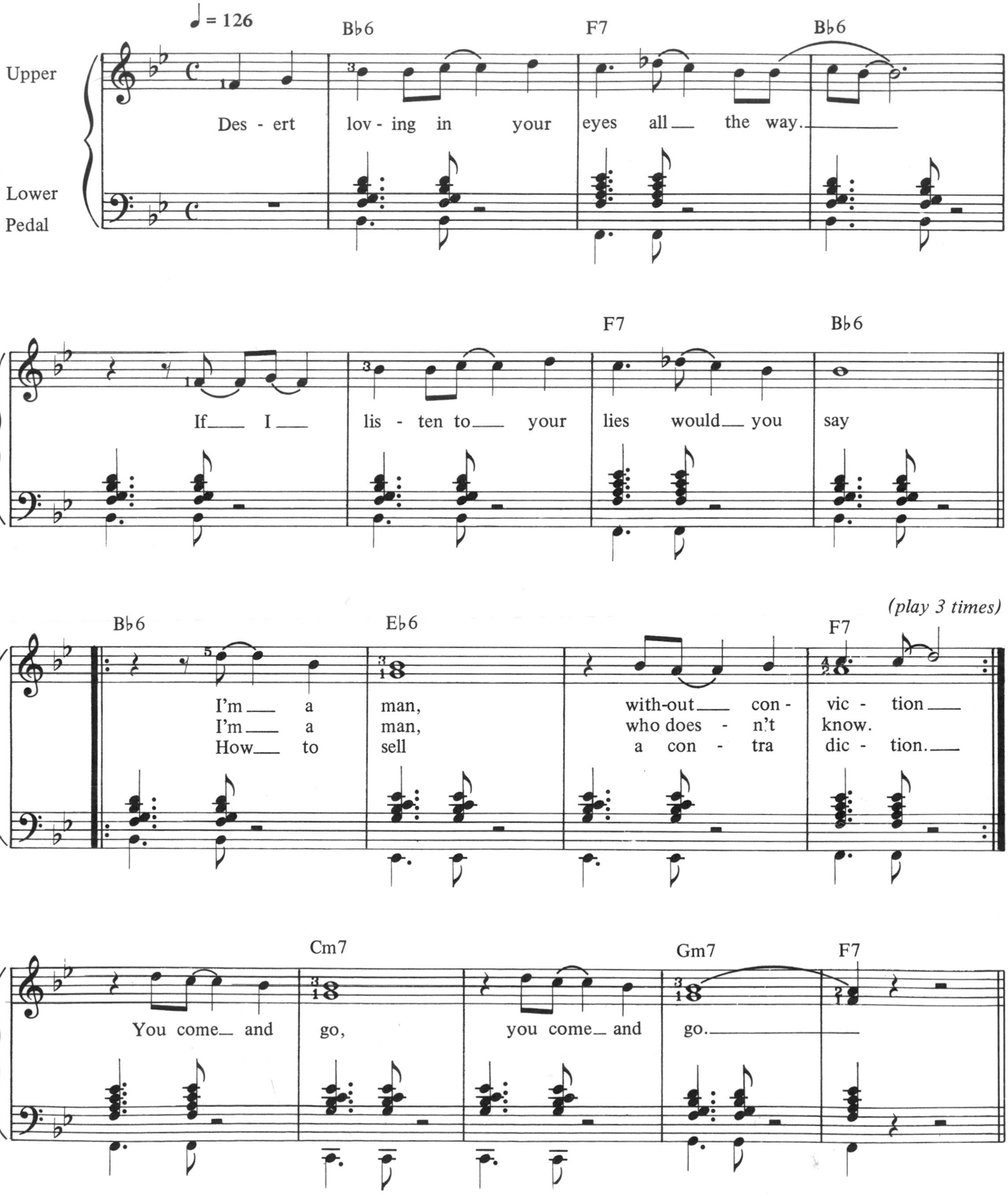

♩ = 126
Upper
Lower
Pedal
Bb6
F7
Bb6
Des - ert
lov - ing in your
eyes all the way.
F7
Bb6
If I
lis - ten to your
lies would you
say
Bb6
Eb6
(play 3 times)
F7
I'm a
man,
with-out con -
vic - tion
I'm a
man,
who does - n't
know.
How to
sell
a con - tra
dic - tion.
Cm7
Gm7
F7
You come and
go,
you come and
go.

CHORUS

Karma Karma Karma Karma Karma Chameleon

loving would be easy if your colours were like my dream.

You come and go,

Red, gold and green.

You come and go.

Red, gold and green.

MIDDLE

Ev'ry day is like survival.

You're my lover not my rival.

ON THE WINGS OF LOVE

Words: Jeffrey Osborne
Music: Peter Schless

Registration No. ⑧
Suggested Drum Rhythm: **Bossa Nova**

ANGELA (THEME FROM 'TAXI')

By: Bob James

Registration No. ③
Suggested Drum Rhythm: **Bossa Nova**

SUDDENLY

Words & Music: Keith Diamond and Billy Ocean

Registration No. ①
Suggested Drum Rhythm: **Disco (or Rock)**

EASTENDERS (THEME FROM)

By: Leslie Osborne and Simon May

Registration No. ②
Suggested Drum Rhythm: **Rock**

REILLY (THEME FROM)

Based on "Romance" by Shostakovich
Arranged by: Harry Rabinowitz

Registration No. ④
Suggested Drum Rhythm: **Bossa Nova**

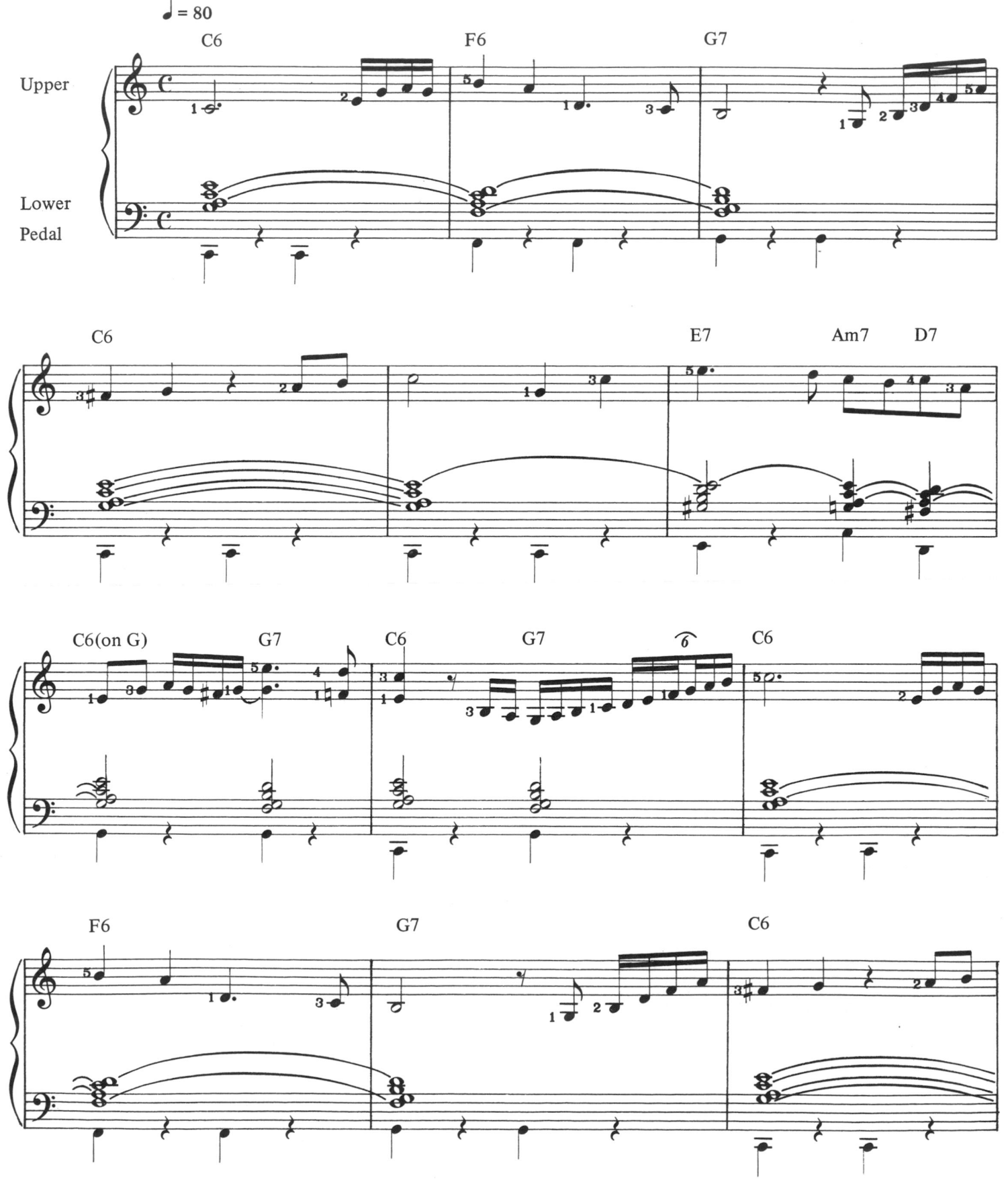

*C#º, with G pedal

UPTOWN GIRL

Words & Music: Billy Joel

Registration No. ⑤
Suggested Drum Rhythm: **Rock**

I KNOW HIM SO WELL

Words & Music: Benny Andersson, Tim Rice and Bjorn Ulvaeus

Registration No. ④
Suggested Drum Rhythm: **Bossa Nova**

But it took time to un-der-stand the man. Now at least I know I know him well.

Was-n't it good? Oh so good!__ Was-n't he fine? Oh so fine!__ Is-n't it

mad-ness, he can't be mine?__ But in the end he needs a lit-tle bit

more than me, more.__ He needs his fan-ta-sy and free-dom, I know him so

well.

THAT OLE DEVIL CALLED LOVE

Words & Music: Doris Fisher and Allan Roberts

Registration No. ⑦
Suggested Drum Rhythm: **Swing**

BALLADE POUR ADELINE

Composer: Paul de Senneville

Registration No. ③
Suggested Drum Rhythm: **Bossa Nova**

A ROCKIN' GOOD WAY (TO MESS AROUND AND FALL IN LOVE)

Words & Music: Brook Benton, Luchi de Jesus and Clyde Otis

Registration No. (5)
Suggested Drum Rhythm: **Rock**

CHORD CHARTS (For Left Hand)

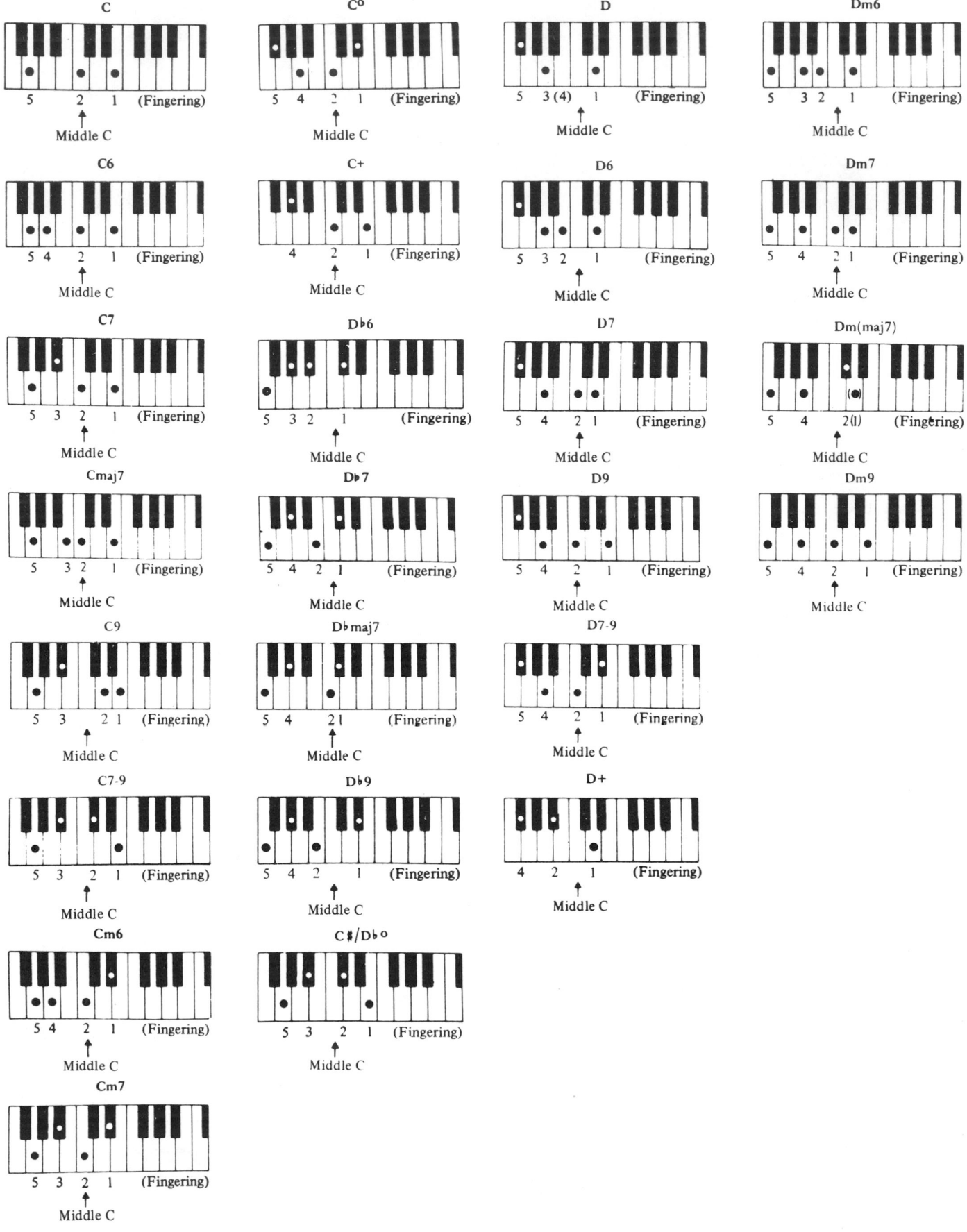

44

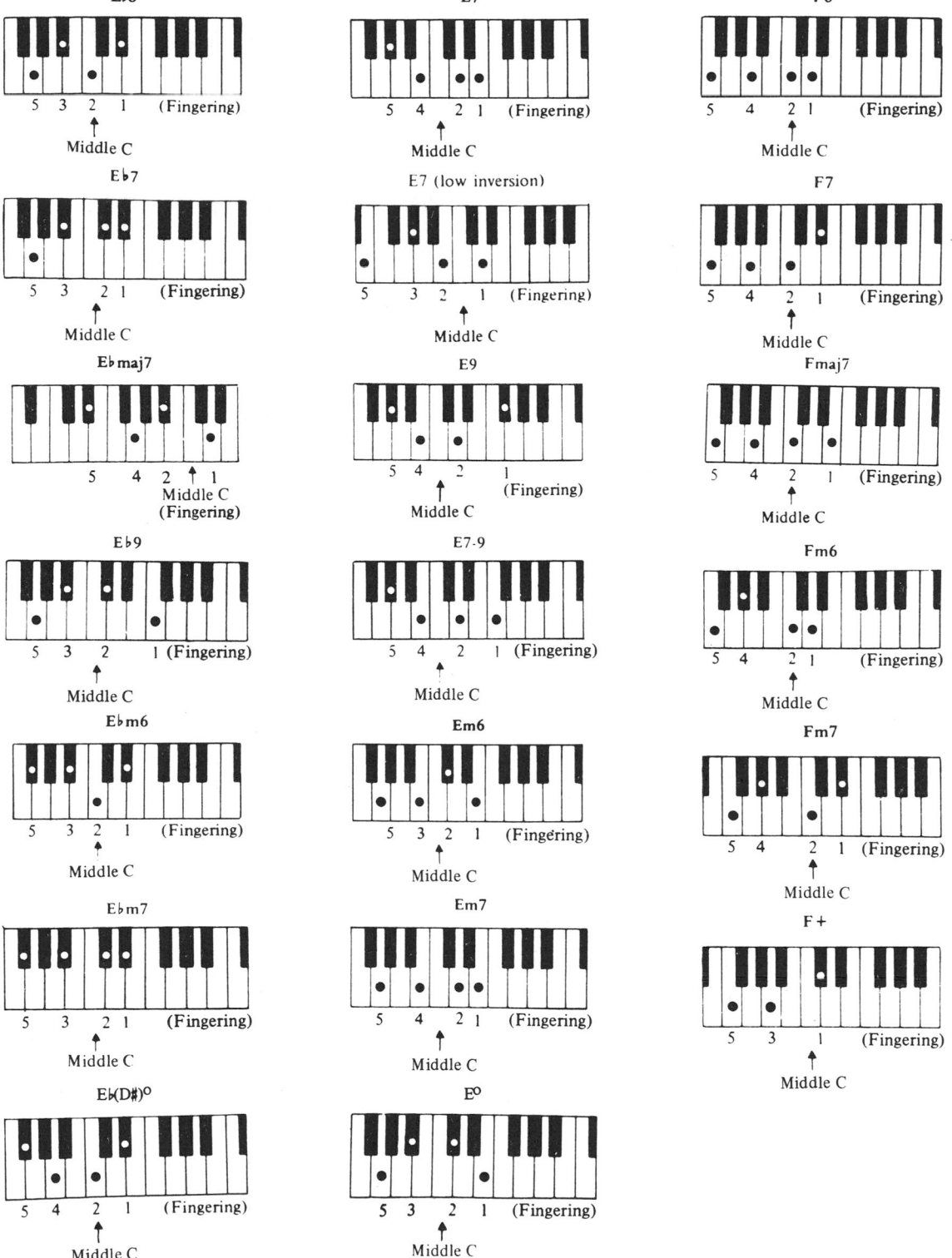

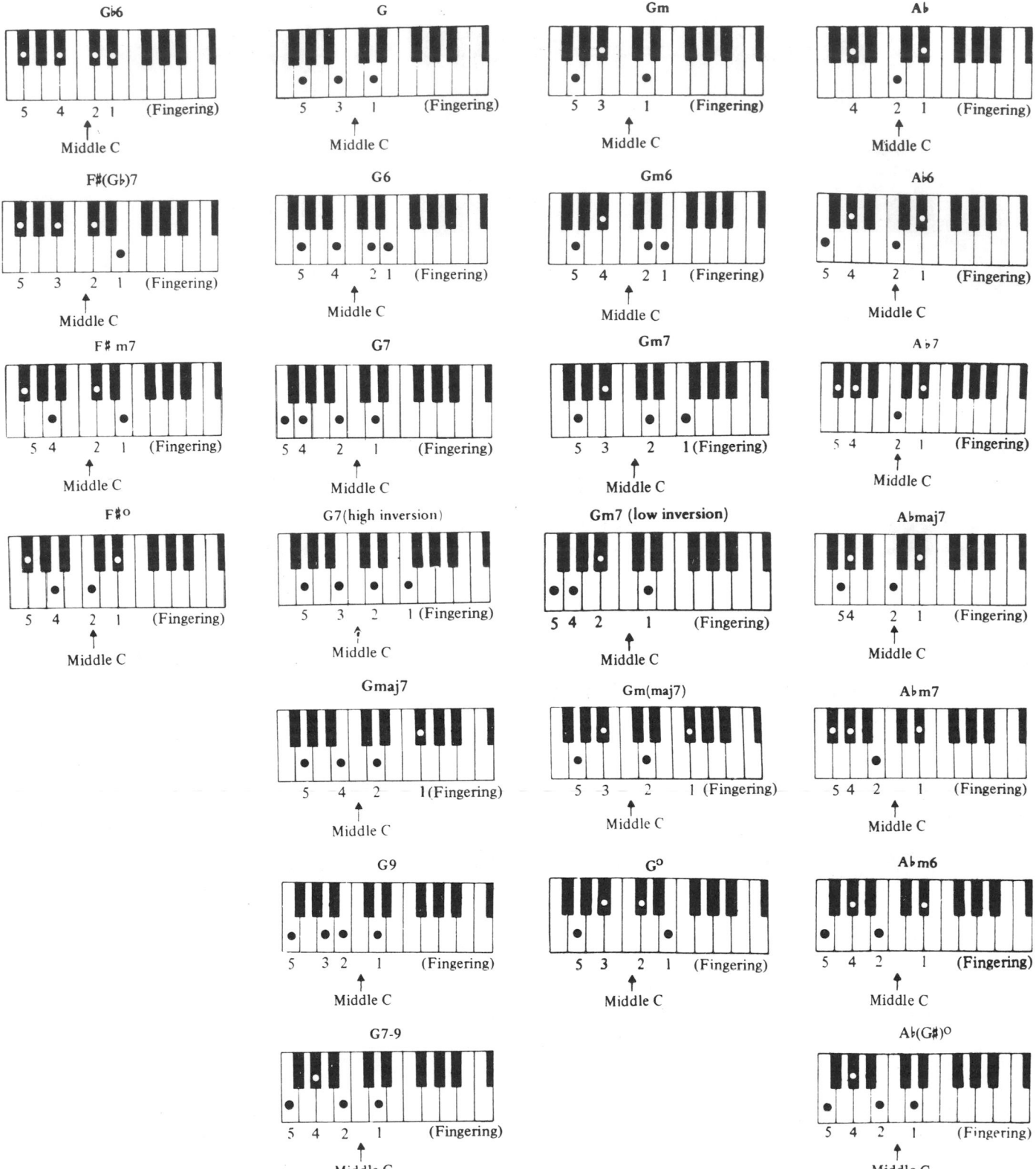

46

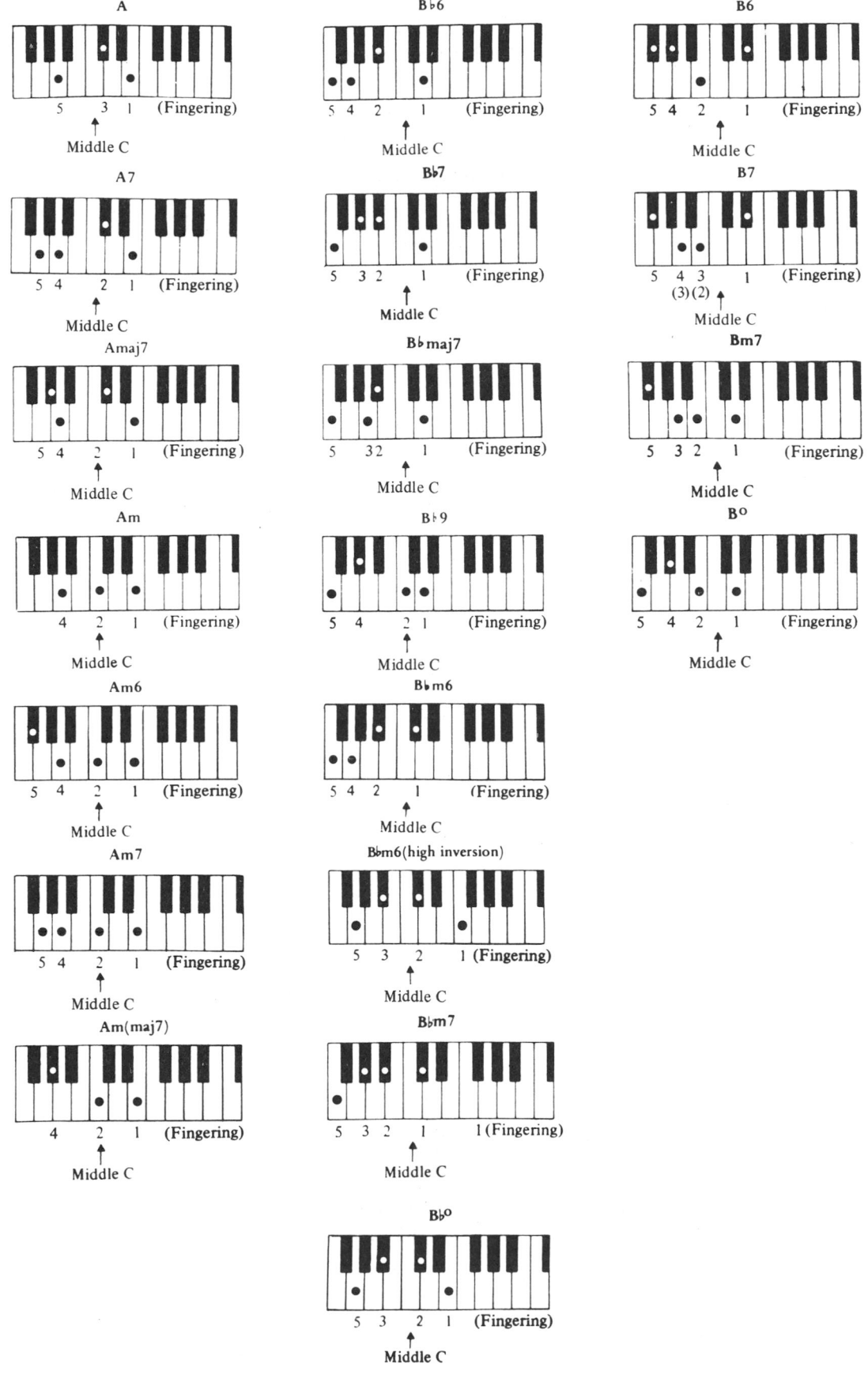

47

ARTISTS

T.V. MUSIC